CW01346181

GANGSTA RAP FOR THE YOUTH

The Things They May Not Tell You
about Crime and Street Life

By: David K. Hudson

"The Young Person's Guide to Self Empowerment"

Order this book online at www.trafford.com
or email orders@trafford.com

Most Trafford titles are also available at major online book retailers.

© Copyright 2011 David K. Hudson.

All rights reserved. No part of this publication may be reproduced, stored in a retrieval system, or transmitted, in any form or by any means, electronic, mechanical, photocopying, recording, or otherwise, without the written prior permission of the author.

Printed in the United States of America.

ISBN: 978-1-4269-8891-2 (sc)
ISBN: 978-1-4269-8890-5 (hc)
ISBN: 978-1-4269-8889-9 (e)

Library of Congress Control Number: 2011913733

Trafford rev. 10/29/2011

Trafford PUBLISHING   www.trafford.com

North America & international
toll-free: 1 888 232 4444 (USA & Canada)
phone: 250 383 6864 ♦ fax: 812 355 4082

Contents

Dedication	....	vii
Acknowledgments	....	ix
Introduction	....	xi
Life Is Choices	....	1
Things They May Not Tell You	....	7
Visitation	....	12
Real Talk	....	18
The Age of Consent	....	22
So You Wanna Become A Stripper?	....	27
Who Do You Believe In?	....	38
About The Author	....	43
<u>Conclusion:</u>	....	53
Special Thanks	....	55
In Memory Of…	....	57

Dedication

To the young people of the world who do not believe that they possess the power and the will within themselves to make right choices; to the youth who feel that they are victims of their circumstances, environment, family structure or lack of, these words will assure you that you and you alone have the power of choice from within.

To all victims of crime

I owe nothing to the living but respect. To those who have passed on I owe the truth.

To our family's youth

To my nephews, Petrius Hudson, Sabien Hudson, Tyrone Bills and Ronnie Phillips; my nieces Bianca R. Hudson and Sydney Hudson; my great nieces Endia Soniae and Madison Cloud.

Programs and Organizations

To the Youth Deterrent Program at Ryan Road Correctional Facility, Detroit, Michigan; Operation Reach, Saginaw, Michigan; Community Action Porteros, C.A.P.S. Inc.; and Fathers Incarcerated Needing to be Dads, "F.I.N.D. Inc.; to all choices made in youth and group Homes, Juvenile and Prison Facilities throughout the world.

Acknowledgments

To The Author, The Creator, The Governor of the world; almighty, eternal, and incomprehensible. To You alone do I owe thanksgiving, admiration and praise. Like "Footsteps" in the sand, you've carried me.

To my loving, devoted and caring, wife, partner, best friend, and inspiring mentor. You have dared me to do wondrous things and shown what true love really means. Your fidelity and tenacity are remarkable. I am in debt to you in this life and after. No words can explain how much you mean to me. You'd say "words are a good start" (smile). " I had to lose myself in love so I could love you better."

To our daughters Marie, Ernestine, and Erica Iris, thanks for sharing your treasure with me. I owe you more than you will ever know. To Erica, my reflection, daughter, and motivation for living. Thank you for your unyielding persistence throughout life letting everyone know that I am your Daddy and no situation or circumstances can be my excuse. You held me to a standard of fatherhood that helped mold me into the responsible adult I have evolved into during my incarceration. Thank you for carrying on our bloodline and bringing my beautiful granddaughter TaNylah into this world. Regardless of the circumstances, you've always made my presence known in her life. I commend you on being the mother you've always needed. "NuNu, this one is for you!"

To my oldest brother, Gregory, its time to recreate the power. Pastor Gerald, its truly God's work to give of yourself.

To my sister Beverly. I know your life would be different had I made the right choice that January 29th, night. I pray every day that you gain more strength to live than just exist. Affliction affects our body, but grief can control our minds. Let those precious souls sail on smoother sea. We had our time with mom and Johnnie, now let God.

Tom Adams and Jessica Taylor, Chance for Life Corporation, you gave me the road map to transformation. "Tom, you can keep my swagger, Playa" (smile).

To Professor Lora Lempert, University of Michigan and all the Inside Out Program Students. Dr. Lempert, you believed in me from the start and gave me the courage to write. No more red marks! To Professor William Tregea, Adrian College. You inspired me to write about my life's experiences in your workshop classes. Once I saw your book of my writings, I was empowered to contribute more. This is your work just as well as mine. Thank you all for caring and enduring all the delays to come in to see me. To all my College and University Professors mentioned in the "About the Author".

Introduction

The concept for this book has been in the works for my entire life. The actual manuscript was written between 3:00 to 5:00 A.M. over a period of four days. The ideas were overwhelming, I was unable to sleep until I had written down every word that was revealed to me during those hours. Then I would fall into a deep sleep and awake well rested only to be amazed about what was lying before me in print.

From the Dedication to the Memory I can take little credit for the writings you are about to read. I only know that if it has half the changing power on your life that it had on mine, then this work is not in vain. I am confident that I was just a vehicle for the message contained in these writings. As "a courier," my job was to merely deliver the material to its destination. It is your obligation to make these lessons work for you in the best way possible. It is with this understanding that I say, "It's your life, you have the power to make the right choice."

Life Is Choices

"Life is choices!" That is by far the most profound phrase that I have heard since entering the Michigan Penal System nearly 29 years ago.

I was meeting with my Resident Unit Manager "RUM" (counselor) for the first time during a life sentence Parole Eligibility Report (PER) when those words were uttered to me by RUM Virginia Brown at the Western Wayne Correctional Facility. No one had ever told me that my life was the choices that I made.

Ms. Brown spoke those words to me after reviewing my prison file and determining "what a waste of life" it contained. The lives of the victims, their families, my family and my life. My prison file revealed that I was a college student at Wayne State University and Wayne County Community College majoring in Criminal Justice. I had made "a choice" after spending several years as an Arc Welder at Ford Motor Company Dearborn Stamping Plant to return to college. I wanted to pursue a career in law when the automotive industry started to decline in Detroit, Michigan.

It hadn't occurred to me, in the moment RUM Brown made that assertion, that many lives were actually wasted as a result of my actions and "the choices" I made early on in life. Up until that moment, life was all about me and what I thought the world should be. I had little or no serious thought of the effect on other people's lives my selfish actions had taken.

Coming to understand that "Life is Choices," after RUM Brown made that statement. I began on a journey to evaluate, reflect, and alter the choices I made in my life. It was that day – nearly eight years after my conviction, I decided to accept the control over my life that I possessed all along. But I had given up my power of choice, to whatever circumstances that I faced.

At the time of the crime, I was back in the neighborhood after a weekend break from College when I met up with an old childhood homeboy. It was "the choices" I made that January night that sent my life in a totally different direction than I had planned when I enrolled in college several years prior.

The choice I made that January night was to go and get a gun from my college friend's brother for what I believed to be a quick sell and make a profit. My goal was clear in my head, but what I failed to equate was the possibilities of what my "home boy's" goals were. He had the connection to sell the gun to a local drug dealer. That small detail of what his decision might have been was not a factor in what I believed we were going to do. Real talk..., I made the ultimate choice.

I came ro realize in the days after my Parole Eligibility Interview with R.U.M. Brown that circumstances don't make a girl or boy. They simply reveal them to themselves.

As a human being, we all have the ability to make choices in our lives and to direct our life's course. We can make excuses and attempt to place blame on the parent(s) God blessed us with, the neighborhood we were exposed to, the school system, the drugs, the alcohol, our codefendant, "the man", the environment, poverty, siblings, or any other excuses we can muster in our minds to justify our actions. The bottom line is, in all situations, we have the ability to make a choice.

That ability may be, choosing the people you hang with, the music you listen to, the boyfriend or girlfriend you date, the way you communicate, the person you decide to have sex with, the decision to take your first drink, to smoke, what club to party at, what school to attend, what classes to take, what clothes to wear, etc. All the decisions in your daily life are a result of what you think and feel about yourself or any given situation. It is not the result of an outside circumstance. You make the choice and decide on how to react to every situation you face. The power of "right" choices is within you.

In our youthful thinking, we may not consider all the possibilities or the outcome of our actions. It's the self gratification of the moment that seems most pleasurable to us. Regardless of all else, we need what we need, when we need it, and that's by any means necessary! It is this selfishness that helps determine what choices we make in life. Not considering all the possible outcomes can have a devastating affect on our lives as well as the people around us. We must understand that we are all linked together by the choices we make. It often appears that we are alone in the things we suffer or experience, but the bottom line is, there is nothing new under the sun. Whatever we are going through, someone else has had the same or similar experience who may be willing to share outcomes. The choice to calmly share your concerns is all that may be required.

The excuses of placing blame on the circumstances, person you're with, parents, your environment, "the man" or what I consider... the "because of syndrome" is no reason to make the wrong choice, (ex.: I beat her down because of...I shot him because...I stole it because...) At any given moment, the choice is yours! Choosing to use violence (use of physical force with the intent to injure), selling drugs, joining a gang, disrespecting your parents (or any elder), stealing, robbing, experimenting with drugs, alcohol, or whatever circumstance you face in your daily life is your choice to make. The ability to choose is within your power. In most cases, no outside situation can dictate the choice you make. When someone steals from you, to avenge your loss, you get a gun, knife, or fight to compensate for your loss, to make things even. Well, the financial investor (Donald Trump, Warren Buffet) may lose hundreds of thousands of dollars in a single deal, but never resort to the use of physical force with the intent to injure. That is because, the investor made a choice. You have the ability to make that same choice. If you want to be a millionaire, make millionaire choices.

David K. Hudson

The ability to make "right" choices is what makes a youth a productive adult and faithful member of society. It is not in our wise ability as male or female to point guns in another teens face to solve disputes, cyber bullying, sell drugs to buy the latest fashions or seek temporary gains claiming to provide for our family, and then say that makes us responsible adults. Growing into responsible adults means making "right" choices when we're young regardless of our circumstances.

When certain rappers are robbed for their jewelry, or suffer the loss from their home getting broken into, they do not resort to violence. The right choice early on to buy insurance was the responsible choice to recover their loss. Getting four thousand dollar rims on your hoopty in a "financially challenged" or modest neighborhood where you live with your parents is not the right choice for longevity and the economy of future wealth. Next year a new set of spinners will be produced and another five thousand dollar price tag placed upon them. Chasing car parts is like chasing gym shoes. The latest pair is only as good as the advertisement date of the next model.

As youths, you must began to make choices that are rational and beneficial to the progression of your life as an adult. Not thinking just "to feel – in the moment". Needing the latest fashion is a self esteem issue. It's not a popularity contest.

That's a Wow Moment isn't it? One of those moments that makes you say! Wow, I never thought about that! Or no one has ever put it that way! Self esteem requires examining your true self worth, not trying to compensate your worth by the latest label on your butt cheeks or chest. Needing the latest labels on your breast or bottom is a self esteem problem, not a popularity contest.

I was watching BET's 106 & Park Show on my flat screen television set. During a particular segment the most popular rapper at the time, Eminem was asked the question. Where is your bling bling? (Expensive Jewelry). Sean Puffy Combs, Nelly, and Plies had been on the 106 & Park Show with jewelry in the range of several million dollar (4 mill for Nelly and 2 mill for plies)

What Eminem said was a "Wow Moment" for me. When asked by host Roxy about his lack of bling, he stated "I have better things to do with my money than to buy expensive jewelry. I have two daughters that needed to attend college." I was so enlightened hearing those words come from the one rapper who changed the financial market of record sales in the "recessed" rap industry. Em was not swayed by the customs or latest fashions in the rap world. Yet, he is our "favorite rapper" and out sold every other rapper in the industry in every given quarter of sales tally. Eminem could have easily said that his expensive jewelry was at home or back stage with his assistant. But he made the choice to use his profits from his explosive record sales to invest in his daughters' futures. One of them is not actually his biological daughter, but his ex-wife's and her one time drug dealer boyfriend's daughter. Eminem made the choice to be a father to both girls and provide for them to have a better future. Even in his youth, he had a controversial situation or two, but nothing fatal. We are all aware of his upbringing and the problems he so eloquently publicized in his music. Even though Marshal Mathers may have had a questionable relationship with his mother and never really knew his father, those circumstances did not affect his ability to be the best parent he possibly could be. His bout with prescription drugs and public divorce only made him more determined to make better choices and be the productive citizen society expected him to be. I imagine he had some pretty good role models and handlers in his camp that contributed to his new outlook on life. That is a primary reason why I chose to share this real talk with you. We all need someone who's been there and done that to share their experience without the glamour and glitz.

As youths, you need to get the true story and weigh the facts for yourself in your own mind and time. The choice you made to read this book is the first step in regaining your power and accepting the responsibility to be a productive member of society. We don't need to make excuses or explain our actions away with the circumstances we face on a daily basis. Whenever in doubt about what to do, you should make the choice to do nothing until you afford yourself the opportunity to explore all alternatives or options. If you have doubt, it may not be the right choice. Your very nature as a youth is to do good, oftentimes it's your second guessing that determines otherwise.

The entire world was created for you to venture into. What's happening in your school, in your family, on your block or in your community is no reason to make the wrong choices. If most people are doing something, it can't be that special anyway. I know peer pressure can make it seem like you're not "in with the crowd." However, with today's technology, you can explore the world from your finger tips and know that what is happening on your block or in your city may not be what is happening in college, private school, or neighborhoods around the world. There is no reason for any youth to feel left out. Making the right choice should be your foremost option. In order to determine the right choice, consider the rules of society. Most decisions in contradiction to those rules could very well be the wrong choice.

If you have problems figuring out the rules, check with a responsible parent, a responsible sibling, uncle, aunt, college law library, a genuinely concerned teacher, a mentor, a divine minister, a responsible priest, pastor, a temple leader, a responsible church member, the police officer driving the streets, or a responsible adult. Whatever you may think you're going through is nothing new. "Been there done that", is what a responsible adult is going to share with you.

Only time changes, people and situations primarily remain the same. It's our ability to cope and deal with those situations that make the difference.

You have the ability to make all the correct choices and do what's within your power. If there is anything we have control over – it is the choices we make and how we react to any given situation. That is within your grasp, never give it away!

Your future happiness depends on the present choices you make. Make a life of right choices and avoid the trap of incarceration. Stay focused, work towards your dreams, then watch your goals unfold right in front of you. It's the age old formula that's tested and proven. Nothing is new under the sun.

Things They May Not Tell You

Under the 13th Amendment of the U.S. Consitution, 1.

Slavery abolished. It states:

Section 1. *Neither slavery or involuntary servitude, except as a punishment for crime whereof the party shall have been duly convicted, shall exist within the United States, or any place subject to their jurisdiction*

In short, if you have been convicted of a crime, you are subject to slavery. In this world of advanced technology you are a slave under these provisions of the Constitution if you have been duly convicted of a crime.

With the U.S. Government's backing of slavery, a state can and does limit your rights as an incarcerated citizen. Your rights are limited to First Amendment Rights of Speech, Association (visits), Religion; Fourteenth Amendment Right to Due Process; and Eighth Amendment Right to Cruel and Unusual Punishment (adequate medical care, food, proper ventilation, and adequate living conditions).

In your daily life as a state prisoner, the street life creed often omitted to give you the game on the affects of prison life. The life that affects you, your girl, mom, dad, brother, sister, your man, cousins, aunts, uncles, and all the ones you love. Be assured, being sent to prison will show you the ones who truly love you and separate those <u>you</u> believe loved you. Your entire system of belief and faith in people will undergo an extreme reconstruction in a matter of months, years and sometimes even days.

Simple things like walking to the refrigerator getting a cold glass of ice water, going to the store to purchase your favorite beverage of choice, a snack, even going to the mall or movie will be a distant memory. The treasure of lying in bed on your Serta mattress making joyful phone calls to your friends or texting them at midnight with a thought or problem is no longer an option. You traded that for "three hots and a cot with a different sexual orientation on every rock."

The nagging from your mother, bickering with your sister or brother will be moments you look back on and think of how trivial the issues really were. You only wish you would have been more thoughtful of what they desired and open to the point they were attempting to express. You will long for the moments to hear a certain loved ones voice, or to make love to the woman or man of your desires.

Very few of the simple pleasures you enjoy as a free teenager will be available to you in prison. Prison creed: "You have no knife, you have no gun. Now you will remember, you're momma's son."

The joy of riding in a car, cruising the park, parkin' lot pimping, clubbin', hanging with the people you enjoy the most. These are the things you forfeited that the street Boss will not share with you when you're in his "spot" selling his drugs, robbing, stealing, carjacking, or whatever illegal hustle is second nature to you today.

Throughout your criminal activities, the drawbacks of your deeds are rarely shared or exposed in your favorite rap lyrics. The composers of "poetry put to song" only glorify the street aspects of the game but they never "really give you the game."

The betrayal of your co-dee is unsuspected. Especially when you're arrested and handcuffed to a desk in separate rooms at the local precinct with police running in and out the room playing mind games of "good cop – bad cop" with your brain. You trust the police and believe whatever ounce of evidence they share that your codefendant has "thrown down first." That is – giving his version of events placing all the blame of the street capers on you. Who will be the first to get the better deal? Who will be the weakest link in the chain? Who will spill the beans and prove that honor among thieves is truly just a slick cliché?

None of these small details are explained to you when you're enjoying the criminal aspects of breaking the law. It's a common occurrence in the ghettos of our society and you never get to truly digest the after effects until you are caught. Two hours, two weeks or two years, you will eventually be apprehended. Cold case files are reopened twenty or thirty years down the road. Then you come to realize that you don't have to pull the trigger to be convicted of murder. You don't have to go in the store with a gun and rob to be convicted or armed robbery. Driving the car, looking out, or providing a weapon to a friend is enough to get a life sentence. You don't have to penetrate that girl at the party who you and the fellas call a "bust-o" to be convicted of rape. Just because you held her down while your boy sexually assaulted her means that you are just as guilty of rape as he is under the law. Common sense doesn't come into play with most state laws. "If I didn't have the gun and did not shoot her/him, then why am I being charged with murder?" "I only got the gun out of my father's dresser." That won't help you avoid a lengthy prison sentence under the law. No one shares these things with you. You believe "since it's my first time, I'll only get probations." NOT!

That is the trap of crime and criminal thinking. We never believe because we did not actually commit the offense that we are guilty of the elements. Well, let me enlighten you to the law of Aiding and Abetting.

Under the common law or statutory law of aiding and abetting, you are just as guilty of a crime as the actual perpetrator! If you aid, assist, encourage, induce, or entice, you can be convicted of the offense just as if you actually did it. The law doesn't make those minor distinctions. Shouting words to your partner in crime to "shoot'em" can get you a life sentence. Whether they catch the actual shooter (principle) or not, under the theory of aiding and abetting, you or your homies can be convicted if nobody tells who actually pulled the trigger. Another Wow Moment huh!

I'm not writing this to glorify the rewards of street hustling. You already know that aspect of the game. But no one is going to tell you that the nice car you acquired from drug sales or robbing, the Benz or Beamer, the Six Four, Customized Impala, Hydraulic Grand Prix, or Grand Am with the candy coated paint job is all going to be gone once you're busted. The jewelry, iced out necklace with the platinum medallion, Coogi outfits, True Religion Jeans, Rocawear gear, Sean John, Ecko, Red Monkey Jeans, Dolce and any other designer on your butt cheeks or chest will all be a thing of the past. State Blues and orange shorts with a Wyte Tee will be your attire in state prison.

Lights out at 12 midnight in most cases. If you're in the Youth Facility in Lapeer, Mich., on the milk program , 10 P.M. is your bed time. No late night snacks in the kitchen. No hot meals at your beck and call. Wendy's, McDonalds, Pizza, Chuckie Cheese, Chili Dogs, Double Burgers, Lobster, Shrimp, Chinese Shrimp Fried Rice, Classy Restaurants, whatever you indulged in while getting paid, will be a conversation piece of the "has been." Where I come from, a "has been" is like "never was."

"Never was" will be the thought of you in the streets you loved so much. "I had this, I have been that." The reality now is, you will have nothing and in prison, You've been had is the punchline!

You are viewed as a loser. One who once did it but not here to do it any more. Rap songs by T.I., Young Jeezy, Plies, and Gucci Mane are filled with "has beens." Your girl, is "Sport Coat's" girl now. The sack you had is gone. She chased it while you were free. Now she's Regina's girl. Dialing her number and receiving no answer on the cellphone you brought is a common occurrence. Lifting the prison phone, you hear the instructions of the voice over tell you to press 1. Then press 0 for a collect call or 1 for a debit call. Then the voice says, punch in the area code and the number you are dialing. Waiting what seems like eternity, the voice says, punch in your prison number and the secret four digits you were issued to personalize your 20 number calling list. You are subject to 1 to 2 minutes of this process before any consideration is given as to whether your loved one answers or accepts your call. All this is just another aspect of prison life the street Boss' doesn't tell you.

I have watched several young men just coming down dial a number on these prison phones (15 minutes a call) 20 to 45 times back to back hoping his "dime piece" (girlfriend) will at least pick up.

When no one answers or her "new man" picks up, the miserable reality of crime and its aftermath sets in. Defeated and feeling helpless, the harsh fact of lying on your plastic mattress, two inches thin, with a solid metal slab underneath, with one half inch tall metal railing holding you two and half feet from the floor on four steel pipes is where you'll sulk in anger and regret. Really only mad at yourself.

In a daze, you imagine what your girl is doing? Is she letting my boy ride the waves? Is she partying or clubbing with girls that hook her up with Ballers? You're totally confused as to why she won't answer your calls. You know she keeps her cell phone with her. Stuck in a time warp you're rendered defenseless, frustrated, and bewildered. You have no sense of the time that's passing in the outside world. Only that 17 foot barbed wire fence with rolls of barbed wire stacked between two buffer fences and the one mile radius of the prison compound besieges your entire world. So, "you wanna be a Baller"?

Visitation

If you're fortunate, "your girl" comes to visit on the day before or after the holidays just to appease you in case your conviction is reversed within the first few years, (Sweetest Day, Valentine's Day etc.) Keep in mind she has to spend the actual holiday with her new companion. The one who's now there that gives her or him what you can no longer provide. All those special moments you once shared with your sweetheart. She longs for those times, but you are no longer free to experience that familiar joy. After a while, it makes no difference whether it's with you or not, she moves on. Her life isn't placed on hold because you are no longer available. You chose the drug life and guns. Now you're a convicted felon sentenced to prison.

The time comes when you ask her to visit you. If she agrees, has a good car and can afford the drive you're lucky. You seek out a prison barber to line you up and trim off a few layers on your over grown waves. This may cost 4 Dials or Next 1 Sport Soaps.

But wait, you owe $6,650 dollars in victim restitution ($6,000) and court fees ($650.00). What they didn't tell you is your prison account is flagged your account whenever your mom, sister, or brother sent you $50.00 or $100.00. You only get half of that amount because the other half is taken before the ink is dry on the money order or JPAY.com account you receive. All your money is taken until the court cost of $650.00 is paid in full. This alone will leave you struggling in poverty. Then half is deducted for victim restitution. That equates to you not having a visiting outfit to wear on a visit to see your girl or guy. You can't even afford to purchase the $35.00

car head rest monitor, that the prison appliance ordering calls a flat screen television and charges you $145.00 for. They seldom tell you the poverty you suffer in prison is due to the hidden costs of a felony-conviction. Yeah, that once free defense attorney who sold you out down the river. You owe the county $600.00 for his generous service of representing you.

Oh yeah, the visit is special so you need to borrow your homeboy's Rocawear Jeans and Sean John Polo. But he isn't feeling you like that because he can't get back. You have no money. You take showers with state soap and rarely hit the commissary. So he lends you the old faded Levis jeans and dense cotton – out of shape polo he won in a card game on the prison yard. One of the card players were playing with no loot so he had to ante up his personal belongings in his loss to avoid confrontation. They can be fatal.

You've now showered and await your date with your girlfriend and child. Time passes and the anticipation mounts. You wonder if she's really going to show as she promised? Did something happen to her on the two hour drive up? Did she remember to bring her valid driver's license, and the baby's original birth certificate with your name on it to prove you are the father? These things concern you.

All these questions race through your mind as you await the officer's phone to ring and for him to beckon you to the officer's station for a visit.

Visiting hours generally start around 2:30 P.M. to 9:00 P.M. on weekdays and 9:00 to 9:00 on Weekends. You only get 7 visits per month. Two weekends (Saturday or Sunday depending on the last digit of your prison number, whether it is an odd or an even number).

It's now 4:00 P.M. Sunday evening and your girl said she would be here at 1:00 P.M. You have called at least 7 times but no one answers her cellphone. You called your mom and all she knows is that your guy/girl told her Saturday afternoon she was going to drive up and bring your child to see you. You are assured she would not lie to your mother, they have had a working relationship since your bus ride to state prison.

It's nearly six o'clock in the evening. Count time was at 4:30 P.M. to nearly 5:15 P.M. You had to be on your bunk from that time and no one was allowed to move around in the unit or the yard. With the unit officer's permission, you were allowed to use the community bathroom to relieve yourself, only two guys at a time. In waiting, your hope of a visit has diminished. The excitement and anticipation you had about seeing your girl and child are gone. Your joy has turned to anger, then sadness, and finally disappointment. Time moves on!

The guys all seem to be watching, whispering about your being stood up for a visit. A couple guys asked, are you <u>still</u> waiting? Others ask, is everything all right? But you're not hearing them mentally. You have little or no "kick it" for them. Your thoughts are consumed with all the worldly things you used to do and how you mistreated your loved ones and baby's mom. Regret of getting into this mess engulfs your soul. Your leg starts to swing from side to side as you lay in your pool of self pity. No one ever told you this was part of "the game".

Soon after count clears, the officer's radio blare and he quickly lowers the volume on its external speaker so no one can hear the message being transmitted. Minutes later, you hear the officer close the door and his keys jingling. You have become adept to the sounds of prison life. You know when the keys jingle; walkie talkie's blare; the sound of a radio battery hitting the officer's desk; toilets flush; the sound of how many showers may be in use; any sound out of the ordinary may alert you that something may be happening. Slowly, you are adjusting to the things the street creed didn't tell you, prison life.

As you search your sense of understanding and hearing to calculate the sounds, the unit officer walks on the floor. Stopping at the end of your bunk, he softly calls you by your last name and says, "you have a visit". Bring your ID to the desk and get your pass".

A prison pass gives you authorization to enter certain areas of the prison that are not common areas for prisoners to go. It's proof you have permission to be in that area of the prison. The written pass contains the date, time, the authorizing officer's signature who gave you permission to travel after being cleared through the control center, your name, and your six digit prison number (which is preferably used in prison and more important to staff than your name). Have you figured it out yet?...You're just a number.

Getting the officer's word your visit is there, you spring to your feet, wrestling to get those faded Levis jeans on your legs, up your thighs and fastened around your waist. Several prisoners call your name, another shouts, "it's about time'. Your neighbor reluctantly says in an envious tone, "enjoy your visit." The malice in his voice leaves you suspecting he's not sincere. He really hopes your visit is a disaster and your girl came to say "she's leaving you or tired of driving two hours to see you". You remember all the negative things he said about how girls treat guys once they're locked up. How they get with your boys; have other guys driving your car that you left her so she can visit. Sleeping in the bed, you once shared with her. Keeping the $20.00, one of your half decent street homies may have given her, trusting she will mail it to you.

Your girlfriend has shown your pictures around the hood and convinced everyone she is sticking by you faithfully but your attitude, demands, and 50 questions on her daily whereabouts are overwhelming her. She tells them, she needs a break. In translation, "I need someone to have fun with." But you're not there. Oh yeah, the visit…you rush to get your pass from the officer, show him your ID, and dash across the prison yard in a proud strut to the control center to meet your sweetheart, child, mother, father or loved one.

Upon entering the prison control center, you have to submit your hand written pass and ID to the control center officer, Sergeant or lieutanant,--whichever one decides to take notice that you have been standing at the control center glass window for two minutes waiting to be logged in and cleared to enter the sliding glass doors which lead to the visiting area. Standing in the correctional staff's presence and being ignored makes you realize how insignificant you really are, now that prison is the result of the life you chose. Your wrong choices placed you in this role so don't get upset because no one else is feeling your importance or the urgency you have to see your family. It's all part of "the game". Leave it now, or hate it later? It's <u>your</u> choice!

If you own and wear prescription glasses (no tint), or fortunate enough to be married with a plain gold or silver wedding band (no ice or insignia, priced under $75.00) or possess a prison ordered religious chain, cross, star and crescent, rosary or Star of David, these items must be listed on your pass (priced less than $75.00). The unit officer must verify that you possess these items when you left the unit and are wearing them on your visit. You can't leave the visit with items you didn't possess. Smuggling, jewelry, shoes, drugs or any items will result in another conviction and loss of your visit for three years. That means those slick new Buffalo Cartier frames your girl, brother, or boys are wearing, you can't switch with them when they come to visit you. Now, admire life passing you by and suffer these consequences. It's real, and that's not just talk!

Those Mauer gaters and the latest Jordan Nike Air shoes you hustled to buy in the streets? Forget about them! You are now the proud owner of some "Clod hopper" type black state issued pleather shoes with no arch support or insoles. "Style your butt off Hustler", this is your new world in brief, for the life of crime. Oh yeah, the visit.

Once the control center verifies that you actually have the items listed on your pass, asks for your prison ID card, logs you in, and asked if you are wearing state shoes. Then you can proceed to the sliding glass doors or take a seat in the control center waiting area until the visiting room shakedown officer decides to take notice of you and bring you through the gates. Sometimes it's right away, other times "not so much!" You may be waiting twenty minutes. It all depends on what is going on in the control center gates at that time. There's nobody jumping through hoops for you, you are in prison.

Popping bottles, beckoning waitresses, making it rain in the bars, is not happening. You are a six digit number now and an insignificant being that is rendered helpless. Everything you desire to do is controlled by correctional staff. Simply going to the bathroom will require permission. Getting a meal requires permission. Using the phone requires permission. Using the microwave, you need permission, playing games, basketball, lifting weights, jogging, washing your face, brushing your teeth, taking a shower, speaking at certain times, all, at it's appropriate time, require permission. If a staff member is not feeling you that day, well it sucks to be you.

The visiting room officer finally comes to escort you into the visiting area to see your girlfriend, child or family members. He first asks you to empty your pockets inside out and give him your ID. Next he pats you down from head to toe and asks if you have anything in your pocket. "My pockets are inside out" you reason within yourself. If he finds something, and you lied, forget about your visit. A Smuggling major misconduct is the charge! After that "the hole" is your new sleeping quarters. "Now tell me, you wanna to be a Baller?"

Real Talk

The decision to share this information ("game"), with you has been a labor of mine from the first ninety days I spent in the Wayne County Jail back in 1984.

I had made a commitment to "The Creator" and myself to do something for the young adults who might have been misinformed or even uniformed about justice and crime like I was. I believed that the law was in my favor when I was facing a life sentence for robbery and murder of innocent citizens. The reasoning in my mind at that time was: "I didn't actually pull the trigger that fired the fatal shots. I can not be convicted of Felony Murder and Sentenced to spend the rest of my life in prison. It was my first time ever being in trouble with the law, and on your first time, there is no way the Judge was going to send me to prison for the rest of my natural life. So when I get out of this smelly county, I'm going to work with the at risk youth and explain this whole court and prison concept to them."

The small details of my supplying the gun; lending my participation to make the crime possible; not knowing the Judge didn't have any discretion in sentencing under the Felony Murder Doctrine never seriously occurred to me. Without my participation this crime could have never happened. I never knew that I would be convicted and sentenced to the same amount of time as the principle (actual shooter) and receive a Natural Life Sentence on my first offense.

"Who ever heard of such harsh punishment for a college student like myself who had made the Dean's List in his first two years of college? I functioned in society, worked most of my teenage years; rented my own flat; owned a hoopty; and wore the latest fashions." (Such as, a $300.00 LV Briefcase for college, Mauer Gater boots, Lizard shoes in an array of colors, Bossalini beaver skin hats that matched ('gangsta brim"). In such colors as "Iced" baby blue with a navy blue satin band, black on black brims, and tan with a brown satin band.) I been there, done that! None of that matters in prison.

I was the prime candidate to leave that ole Wayne County Jail and return to my criminal justice classes, giving everyone a first hand account of how the justice system works (Just-Us). Our Criminal Justice class had just toured the Wayne County Jail just months prior to me participating in the robbery murder. I had never seen the inside of a county jail until that day our professor, who just happened to be a Captain of the Wayne County Sheriff's Department, took my classmates and me on that tour.

Walking on the catwalk of the county jail as a student made me wonder how all those guys were able to be in such close quarters with the toilet and sink right in their faces. Paint peeling off the walls, concrete floors, and those unsightly rusted bars obstructing those county detainees view.

I reasoned within myself, that, "I could never be subjected to those type of living conditions. No, that would never happen to me. I would rather be dead than live like a caged animal."

I left the county wondering, "How in the world do they survive?" Who would imagine I would have the answer to my own question without any prior jail experience, that warm summer afternoon?

So, here I am, nearly 29 years into a life prison sentence, still with the goal and aspiration of getting out of prison and saving just one young person's life. Being able to give you "the game" on the pitfalls and the illusive aspirations that crime pays and the misplaced glorification that street life is the route is still within my grasp.

Embracing the reality that I may not receive the privilege to physically be present and speak to you the way I envisioned – as a visual example of what crime and criminal thinking can get you. I am now elevated to putting these experiences on paper, trusting that one young man or woman will read this. Hopefully the naked truth will detour you from the illusionary pursuit of the fast money trail. It does not exist in the real world. The end of that trail is prison and loss of valuable life, family, friends, and any hope or dreams of obtaining the riches you so recklessly are in pursuit of.

There are no easy roads to the pot of gold at the end of the rainbow. For all of us who think that way, our thoughts are similar to that of the ravenous dog crossing a bridge with his bone in his mouth. He views the silhouette of another dog from his side vision and leans over the railing of the bridge to take a closer look at the dog in the water below. The water dog appears to be traveling the same road as the dog on the bridge with an apparent larger bone in his mouth. As the dog on the bridge stares at the dog in the water, he stares back, believing that the water dog's bone is much larger than his. He eagerly desires to obtain it.

In an instant, he drops his bone over the bridge and dives into the cold murky waters without a second thought to take the other dog's bone from the waters. Once he splashes in the chilling waters of the deep river, it occurs to him that it was only his reflection from the sun on the water. The water dog with the larger bone was actually himself. Wet, struggling, and paddling to stay afloat, he realizes he has nothing left. The bone in his mouth has sunk to the deep swells of the river and is lost in the sea weeds and crab grass protecting the river's floor. All of his effort to obtain the greater prize was in vain. He now shivers wet and boneless.

Much like the boneless dog, street life and crime offers us no rewards. The grass really isn't any greener on the other side. It's only a reflection of our base desire to be a better person. We must gain patience through critical thinking and by evaluating all possible options and pursue life's goals by making the right choices. Nothing of value that lasts will come in an instant. Dedication and hard work is the only choice that you must make. Anything else is just plain uncivilized and counter productive to the riches you desire. Now, that's Real Talk! But street life may not tell you this!

The streets do no explain the hardship catching a case plays on your mother, father, sister, brother, and all those you love. You may first tell yourself that you're the one that has to do the time. But that's another false assumption that street life gives. It's rare that you can do your time alone! Family is an essential element of the downside of criminal activity. You will barely be able to exist in prison without family support. Your homeboys from the neighborhood are not going to feel sorry for you up in here. They will help you every once and a while, but when you see some of the more fortunate prisoners getting commissary, receiving the Michigan Department Of Corrections "MDOC" approved vendor "Securpaks" of food and snacks from their family's online care package purchases, and you see prisoners cooking up Ramen Noodles, beef stew, rice, chili, pickles, and nachos all mixed together. You also see prisoners on property calls for radios, underwear, personal white T's, $50.00 low quality tennis shoes, "retail rejected" designer pants and shirts, headphones, ridiculously priced flat screen TV's and over priced MP3/player ($130.00), you will feel the pinch of no family support. You think feeling a need to hustle in the streets to obtain fashion was your motivation, think twice about it in here. The ruthless predators are 10 times as devious and constantly scheming to relieve you of your belongings. "It's a jungle in real time. Now, are you still willing to act like a monkey?"

So when you think you're doing a crime on your own accord, you're forcing your family and loved ones into the perpetual cycle of incarceration by the wrong choices you make. That's if they really got love for you. Are you sure? If not, you will be tested!

THE AGE OF CONSENT

My first encounter with sex is probably most unusual than your average young boy or girl. I was sexually assaulted at the age of nine by an older female cousin. During that time sexual assault was not widely talked about in public the way it is today especially when it occurred within the household by a close family member.

You see, the age of consent to have sex in the State of Michigan is 16. If you have sex with anyone under the age of sixteen, you can be charged with a felony under the law (Statutory Rape).

At the time of the sexual assault on me, my parents had just brought my brother Johnnie and me a set of "drawer beds" from Sears Robuck & Co. Being raised in a family with two parents and four children, with a single income, having your own bed was a privilege that was very rare. Up until that day, I shared a mattress and box spring with my brother Johnnie and my older brother Gregory had his own bed in the opposite corner of the den which my parents had converted into a third bedroom for the three boys of the family.

Getting the brand new drawer beds was exciting. The top bed was stacked over a smaller bed that had wheels and could be pulled out or pushed under the larger bed on top. My brother (R.I.P) and I actually wanted bunk beds, but the drawer beds were more affordable and our parents were the ultimate decision makers.

It was an exciting week for us when those beds arrive. So since the boys were having so much fun, my sister Beverly asked our parents to allow one of our teenage female cousins (R.I.P) to come over and spend the weekend with her. You see, my sister was the only girl in the family and she was often left out or over compensated in certain events or family decisions. So, my mother allowed her brother's daughter to come over and spend the weekend in our family home.

Johnnie and I were bouncing up and down on the new beds having pillow fights and seeing who was able to knock the other off the side of the upper bunk. It was a rough boy's game that only my brother and I would dare to play. A game that resulted in several knots upside his and my head from the bumps on the floor or the old oak dresser my parents had brought from the second hand store. It was not the matching set to our new drawer beds, but we never gave it a second thought.

Having a pillow fight and making loud screaming noises caused my cousin to leave the front porch where my sister was braiding the neighborhood girl's hair. My cousin peeped between the curtain which separated our converted den bedroom from my sister's room. The passage way was too narrow for an actual door. You had to walk through my sister's room to get to the boys bedroom. That was the only way to enter because the outside door led to the back porch and my father had installed a space heater in front of that door to warm our bedroom. The den was an addition built on to the house prior to our family purchasing it, so the basement furnace did not provide heat in that area.

When my brother Johnnie noticed my older female cousin watching us pillow fighting he paused and whispered in my ear, "She's watching you." It was unusual for girls to come in our room because we did not have but one sister in the house. As sons my mother was not considered a girl so her presence was often times expected. For whatever reason, my cousin ended up joining the pillow fighting and my brother eventually left the room. I don't exactly remember the reason he left, but my cousin and I were left on the bed bouncing and swinging pillows. I do remember her falling on top of me and pressing her lips on mine. I was still in my pajama bottoms with no shirt on and the snap on my private part area was no task to unfasten. I didn't realize with all the jumping and playing that I must've been excited.

In an instant, I could feel a tingling in my stomach and the soft wet juices of her body enveloping my privacy. It never dawned on me what was going on and I don't remember whether it felt good or bad. It just felt strange. Like something a 9 year old boy should never feel.

With my eyes darting open and shut, feeling her silky jet black hair falling over my face, on the side of my ears and tingling my neck, I didn't notice my mother standing in the curtains. How long my cousin was humping my frail, slim, frame, is just as much a blur to me as the length of time my mother stood there watching her.

Enraged, my mother grabbed that 16 year old by her hair and slung her developed frame to the floor from the top of those brand new drawer beds my brother and I just recently received. She shouted. "I knew ya'll were to damn quiet back here." "You had to be up to something." I felt a lump in my throat and my heart pound.

My mother ordered my cousin, in no certain terms to get up off the floor and out of our room. She ordered me to put myself back into those pajamas and stay in the room unto she tells me to come out. I pulled my lower bunk drawer bed out and hid between the two mattresses like the family dog who had eaten the freshly baked cake left on the kitchen table to cool for dinner as the family returned from their outing.

Spending time between those mattresses, I wondered what I had done wrong. "Why was my mother upset with me?" I had no clue about the birds and bees, sex, girls, kissing, and making babies. No one ever told me about that! No one ever had the birds and bees talk with me that I eventually grew up hearing about in "the hood."

My father (R.I.P) barely had a third grade education. He grew up in the farmland near Macon, Georgia and was only allowed to go to school when it rained. He often told us this story so I eventually asked him, "Why did you go to school only when it rained?" He said, "Because I could not work in the fields or plow the soil when it rained. So my dad would only allow me to go to school on rainy days."

My mother (R.I.P.) was originally from Paris, Tennessee and hadn't finished high school when I was nine years old. You see, my maternal grandmother had passed away when my mother was just a teenager and she was left to be the mother to her 12 siblings. She was the oldest girl and my grandfather was emotionally absent after his wife passed away leaving him with 13 small children. He had no clue about raising a family and back in those days the woman was expected to manage the household. After my grandmother passed the obligation was thrust upon my mother who was not yet 16 years old. She had no or little experience at such a tender age, but I'm told she learned as she went along.

Therefore, I can only suspect, with one sister in my family diagnosed with polio and rarely left the house on dates, or singles outings, sex education in our home was not a priority. The street creed mistakenly promotes that young boys are expected to be conquerers and to subdue as many girls as possible. It was probably believed in my house that I would receive the sex education from that creed. No one ever talked about what my cousin did to me that day.

After my cousin raped me, I completed my entire summer on punishment, not able to leave the house. I never felt secure about sex or ever talked about it in the house. I became reclusive and shy. My stuttered speech developed and worsened in my youth. I was the object of mother bragging to all her friends about my pretty "brown eyes" at church and other outings. In my shyness I would run behind her dress and hide my face in her thighs so no one could see my face. I was known as "the Hudson boy with the pretty brown eyes."

No one talked about my smarts or ability to dance like James Brown, and imitate Stevie Wonder in song. I had convinced my father to buy me a pair of dark sun glasses from the nickel and dime store

David K. Hudson

(Dollar Store) and I took on the Stevie Wonder character to mask my shame. Hiding behind the dark shades made me feel invisible because nobody could see my eyes and I could see them without feeling looked into in return. It was a protective shield I quickly mastered as a youth.

All I was known famous for was my brown eyes. Shy and with a speech impediment I felt alone, in mental seclusion just moving through life and school as an observer, not a participant. I began destroying things around the house, busting bottles in the road way, and one neighbors' basement windows with a soft ball. Inside our home I was called "Destruct-O." I got into trouble for wearing my dark shades in my classes in elementary and junior high school. Every time my mother would take a pair, I would convince my father to buy me another pair. Soon, I learned to keep a secret pair in a hideout so no one could find them. I was never asked why I needed the dark glasses when the sun didn't shine? Or, asked why I was prone to breaking things. (lamps, ash trays, flowers, chairs, etc.)

So, I can understand and relate to how a young person like you might feel you are an object for pleasure and coming to believe that's all you have to offer. You may have been told, "You have to use what you got to get what you want." So you take your well endowed body parts to the local strip club and "shake what your momma gave you." While the "street ballers and potential shot callers" make those dollars rain down upon your precious temple and sacred womb of motherhood. Well, let me tell you the things they may not tell you about a stripper.

So You Wanna Become A Stripper?

The aspiration of making fast money with your body is one of the oldest professions in American History. It's nothing new under the sun. But ask yourself, "Why do I desire to sell my body and be the object of sexual pleasure with no quality love or substance attached?"

"What is it within my soul that limits my thinking to degrading myself and becoming a servant to strangers with no compassion? What is it that life offers which lifts my spirit and brings me to understand that money alone is not the savior of my emptiness?"

"It is only after I have shamed myself and my loved ones that I discover the confidence in my ability to obtain greater things?"

Now, here's the gangsta's rap…I knew a young girl we'll call "Smoothe Coco". She had a body like Nikki Minaj and was kinda smart in school. She ran track, developed physically ahead of her peer group and completed high school in the Detroit, northwestern area. She was among a small group of close knit girls who went to elementary, junior high, and eventually high school together.

Whatever school one of the 4 girls decided to attend, the rest would enroll in that school also. They all eventually graduated together and attended the prom with matching customized made dresses. So relieved to have made it through high school, the girls wanted to take a break, get jobs, and make money to acquire all the necessary things they dreamed of while growing up. Coco had further physically developed into a woman and was catching the eye of all the high profile drug dealers. Most of the "Street bosses" and their comrades were frequenting strip clubs "Making it rain" and blowing hundreds of dollars popping bottles was the norm. The trinkets of street life was intriguing to Coco. She wanted it too!

It was suggested to Coco that she could make easy money and maximize her potential of obtaining riches among an elite group of drug dealers, if she danced at this particular club on Detroit's Westside. She had all the physical jewels God and her mom blessed her with, "Why not use it to get what she wanted?" Coco thought.

The live music bar had been on the corner of Livernois and Vancouver for over four decades. When strip clubs became popular in the mid to late nineties the local owners conformed this hole in the wall to the street's night life demands. Originally the club catered to the factory workers in the area but now that the auto industry in Detroit was declining, the club's clientele changed to the underground enterprise of the drug world in "The city"(Detroit, Michigan).

Smoothe, pondering the ideal of easy money, entered into the underworld of stripping and hanging with the Bosses of the drug trade. She transformed into the life of a stripper and quickly became popular among the ballers who came to the club.

What the game doesn't tell you is when you become popular in the club as a stripper, the girls you are competing against become envious. It's a competition, make no mistake… The goal is who can obtain the greater riches. So if you're the one to make it to the top, then it's you who has the greater amount of enemies to watch out for.

Your job at the top is multiplied. You have to watch out for your own safety from the potential rapist, as well as the drug dealers and their workers who come to the club. You have to watch out for the robbers who scope you out to see how much money you have taken in for the night. Leaving the club late at night makes you easy prey for the gun toting street hustlers who know robbing you for your money isn't likely to be reported.

Next, you must beware of the owner short changing you for your time on stage or serving drinks. Factor in your fellow dancers back stabbing, stealing your property left in the clothing room, "Spiking" your drink, and other ways of "Getting back" unimaginable. You're the competition now, so no rules apply. It's cutthroat, get down at all cost! You know how the street "B's" do it. That's who you wanna be right?

Coco came in the strip club game making the cheddar. She was able to soon move out of her mother's home because her mom did not appreciate what she was doing, coming in all hours of the night, if she came in at all. Her mother became very concerned about her daughter's well being, but Smoothe Coco had it all down pack. She was now in control and could handle her business.

The evenings on the pole had given her false confidence convincing herself she was invincible…unable to hear what the people who truly loved her were saying. Even her childhood girl group she grew up with was confused and didn't know why Smoothe Coco had abandoned their group, and embraced, so gallantly, the night life of stripping. No one could get through to her, she wasn't hearing it.

The money was just too good and allowed her the independence she so passionately desired as a junior and senior in high school. The ability to do what she wanted to do, unrestricted by parental rules and the regulations of her mother…the thought of being a stripper was to enticing and overwhelmed her judgment. She was well beyond the point of making all the wrong choices.

Smoothe Coco, through the short complimentaries of stripping, was able to rent her own apartment and began furnishing it just the way she wanted. A 72 inch screen television, canopy princess bed, the latest technology in music equipment, a wireless laptop, all the things an eighteen year old thought she might want. She could entertain any man of her pleasure who chose to enter her private abode, regardless of his age or martial status, if, she even knew it. No, her mother was no longer allowed to regulate how she lived, who she entertained or how she chose to live. Coco felt free!

After several months in the club, she caught the eye of one particular drug dealer named Dude who had "Come up" and moved his personal residence out "The city". He was international now, moving "Bricks" (Kilos of cocaine) through California, Texas, Minnesota and Ohio. Smoothe Coco had been an object of his desire since her popularity had grown in the club. He never really took her seriously before because she wasn't known throughout the local strip scene. He had a number of girls in clubs he visited all the time, but always strove to conquer the best in "The game". Eventually, in his need to run things, he began spending hundreds of dollars on Coco, picking her up for work and driving her back to her apartment in the finest of automobiles, Lexus, Convertible Corvettes, Cadillac Escalades and a Benz, dressing her in the top latest fashions. She gave little thought to the fast rule of the stripper game and that's "Protect yourself at all times and don't take your job home with you."

Smoothe Coco, was still enjoying the benefits of other Ballers at the club, but Dude was beginning to require more of her time because he was spending the biggest stack of street cheddar on her. She was excited about all the attention and money flowing her way which seemed so effortless. All she had to do was shake her butt, rub her breast and say whatever she thought a Baller needed to hear.

Dude was beginning to demand more of her time and attention because he suspected that his street competitors were sharing his prize. This started to weigh on his ego as he sat in the VIP section of the club and watched Coco dance and mingle with his rivals. She was enjoying the benefits of having Dude and the other ballers ravish her G-string with cheddar, shower her with precious jewels, and shopping sprees at up scale malls in Birmingham and Troy, Michigan. Dude's demands for her to stop dancing and spending time with other Ballers was a decision Smoothe Coco wasn't ready to make. She reasoned, "Who would pay my bills or my $550.00 a month rent?"

Giving up the nightly access to the elite street Players was incomprehensible. But to "Dude" her continuous exposure to his rivals made him look soft. After all, it was mostly his hustling dollars going on a stripper whom he couldn't control. Something had to give! So eventually he made her an offer to get out the strip game.

Dude offered Coco the opportunity to be a "Kept woman". The offer was if she would quit dancing, he would take care of all her needs, pay her bills, pay the $550.00 in rent on her high rise downtown Detroit apartment, maintain her lifestyle and shopping sprees she presently enjoyed. For the first time, Smoothe seriously comtemplated giving up her night life occupation. Although she had heard similar empty promises before, she had started feeling Dude and was digging his swagger. Smoothe asked Dude to allow her time to think about it. He sensed her weakening!

A few weeks had passed since Dude made the proposition to Smoothe Coco. He told her he had to go out of town and when he came back, she needed to make a decision. He dropped 10 thousand he just stacks on her to hold her over until he returned. She agreed to that time frame because Dude had also recently purchased a brand new Pontiac Solstice GXP for her to drive. It was her favorite colors, money green with a tan rag top and interior. She had more independence and was able to drive back and forth to the strip club, and show off to her childhood girls while he was on the road. She had been thinking about his offer, trusted he would keep his word since the car was the perfect start. Not to mention, the 10 stacks he just dropped on her without blinking an eye. She figured, he must be stacking if he gave her 10 grand just like that. In her head it was a no brainer, but the "Man woman street games" shall be carried out.

Two days after Dude took his crew on the road to expand his enterprise in a small town in the upper Midwest, a huge ruckus erupted in the strip club. Bullets soared over Smoothe Coco's head, the sound of gun fire pierced her ears as she dove to the floor while on stage.

Falling down at first, all she could think of was, "These fools done messed up my dance set". Then the loss of her life quickly became her only concern.

An under cover police operation turned into a huge gun fight inside the club. Several people were shot and two died in the Melee. It was a scene Coco had never experienced or expected inside the club. The huge bouncer had given her security. It was reported on the local news and in the newspapers. The drama was enough for Coco to accept Dude's proposition to become a "Kept woman."

Everything was going as promised for the first six months. Since Dude was the only one Coco was dating, she stopped using condoms and began to have unprotected sex with him. He had been discussing having a baby with Coco and assured her that taking care of it would not be a problem. She dreamed of having her own little Dude.

Coco had all her needs met by Dude so she wanted to please him in every way she could to maintain her lifestyle and keep "Her man." She could think of no other way to secure her status as a "Kept woman" than to produce Dude's child. After all, he was still getting uninterrupted tax free dollars. No known Federal indictments.

They spent weekends in Las Vegas, a week in Hawaii, Jamaica, New York, Atlantic City, dining in the finest restaurants, any nineteen year old could only imagine. She often thought to herself, "This is the life I was born to live."

Her girl childhood group was glad the stripping days were over, but envious of her new carefree lifestyle. They visited just to cuddle in her latest fashions, which she so carelessly allowed to borrow or gave them a piece or two.

Eventually Coco got pregnant and gave birth to a beautiful baby boy. Dude seemed so proud he had a junior to carry on his name. Just barely twenty years old Coco didn't have the slightest clue of what motherhood entailed. Her entire life had been about her, and what she wanted. She never had to make any sacrifices or offer any genuine obligation to any other human being. Especially one who could not survive or care for himself without her.

As the added responsibilities grew, in her frustration of motherhood, she felt Dude was just as much obligated for the care of their baby as she was. She concluded, the late night cries, feedings, and diaper changes were his job as well as hers.

Never shy of demanding what she wanted, she began confronting Dude on what she perceived as the neglect of his duties as a father. Dude became frustrated and angry over Coco's demands and questions as to why he only spends half the night, a couple days a week in her bed. He also rarely cared for the needs of their son and spent less time at their high rise apartment. She complained that he wasn't leaving enough money to maintain her lifestyle and provide for their child. He would fire back and tell her to "Quit wasting the money on clothes and jewelry and spend it on the baby."

Her motherly nature was not developed enough to make those changes yet. She felt he broke his promise to make her a "Kept woman." So her anger and disappointment mounted. She would allow anyone who asked to keep the baby, come get him, or she would drop him off so she could go clubbing or shopping at the mall. Her selfish instincts were longing for the gratification of "The street hustle" once again. The life and intensity of the hustle was beckoning its call. Not making the "Right" choice, Coco was willing to obey the circumstances of her negative environment at the expense of her obligations to motherhood.

Her mother soon took "Street custody" of her child. With street custody, her mother had no legal rights or ability to make medical decisions or a tax write off as a parent.

Coco's mother knew her daughter was not ready for what she herself was not prepared for twenty-one years ago. A single parent raising a child! The family cycle had begun to repeat itself.

Dude recognized the "Fiendish street call" in his new baby's mother and decided it was time for Coco to start earning her keep, and stop her from nagging him about what he's not doing.

"If I took the risk, hell everybody was fair game," so thought Dude. She was assigned a task in her baby daddy's street enterprise of transporting a rental car full of drugs from one state to another.

Smoothe did the driving by herself and was trailed by Dude's workers in other vehicles to protect the shipment and assure its proper delivery. She served two purposes, driving and assuring quality delivery without the bricks being chipped from or cut. If someone rode in the car with her, she would have to divide the $2,000 traveling reward with them. She was too selfish and greedy to share anything. It was her mission to eat the entire pie. No matter how bitter the crust. The risk was just a mere passing thought. She had it all figured out, so she imagined.

After several successful trips and enjoying the fruits of her street labor, "Smoothe" again became confident in her ability to out wit authorities and survive in the drug trade. She adapted to the street life no matter what aspects it entailed. The rush of the risk was gratifying in itself.

On a couple of missions, she placed her son and his car seat in the drug car to throw the highway patrols off and render them unsuspecting of her drug transports. This was the perfect caper, in her mind, - "Hell, I may as well put the kid to work. He gets the benefits of the money also. Ain't no free rides in this business." That is how she justifies placing her son at risk in her mind.

While making a trip through Ohio, "Smoothe Coco" came upon a traffic jam in bumper to bumper traffic. The drug protection cars traveling with her were stranded in the far lane a couple cars behind. The drug crew drivers were trained to never travel directly behind the "Spot car" or in the same lane, to avoid a convoy on state highways out of town. Patrol cars can easily detect several license plates of out of state drivers traveling in a convoy with no luggage rack or families in the vehicle. That is just one type of drug transporting profile they are trained to investigate. But on this trip, an Ohio driver was not expecting the sudden stop "Smoothe Coco" was forced to make and did not slam on her brakes in time to avoid hitting the back of the "Spot car". Coco's life flashed before her eyes.

"The spot car" was sent slamming into a car in front and a highway cruiser was in clear vision of the accident because it was parked on the shoulder of the highway in the opposite direction. In the highway patrol car was the K-9 unit with a drug sniffing dog inside. Concerned about the occupants of the vehicles in the collision, the officer immediately swung his police cruiser across the median to secure the area. The protection drivers could see all the activities and immediately phoned Dude to relate the events. The officer had noticed the plates on several cars and brought the dog to sniff for drugs once he discovered that no one was seriously hurt. The protection cars were ordered by Dude to continue the drive to avoid suspicion. Coco was paid enough to fend for herself. "She knew the risk and took them."

"Smoothe Coco" was arrested for possession and interstate transportation of drugs. It was a federal offense once the FBI Drug Task Force discovered who Smoothe Coco was working for.

The task force had been conducting an investigation on Dude for the last year or so and had several pictures and a complete history on Smoothe Coco's activities within the organization. She was destined for federal prison regardless of it being her first time being arrested.

After making bond, she returned to her apartment and saw even less of Dude. He couldn't trust her now and didn't want to jeopardize the remaining assets of his business. Coco had now become a liability, in the drug trade. She was to be avoided at all cost. No one was sure if she was working with the Feds or not. Why would anyone in "The game" take the risk? There are thousand more young girls or guys just like you and Smoothe…misinformed, disillusioned, and unsuspecting of the result of a wrong choice.

Not knowing what getting busted meant in the drug game, Coco didn't understand why Dude would not talk to her. He had his phone numbers changed, quit visiting his son and paying the bills and rent on her $550.00 a month apartment. In a few short months, she was forced to move back home with her mother and found out the car Dude gave her was leased and was reported stolen due to non payment. She had to turn the car in.

In passing weeks, Coco met one of Dude's ambitious crew members and pleaded with him for Dude's new phone number. Coco started blowing up Dude's Smart phone once she conned ole boy for the digits. One late night, a mature sounding woman answered and identified herself as Dude's wife. That nearly brought Coco to tears on the phone. Dude had been married for nine years to a woman much closer to his age 36. They had five children together and lived in a $900,000 home in Grosse Pointe, Michigan, an exclusive upscale neighborhood, one of the riches communities in Michigan. Coco never had a clue of Dude's secret life of marriage! She felt used, betrayed, and enraged. She regretted selling herself cheap!

After several rounds with Dude's wife over the phone, Coco did all she could to avoid a physical confrontation with his wife's female crew. They had found out Smoothe Coco had a baby by Dude and was determined to issue her a royal beat down or possibly a trip to the Wayne County Morgue. Smoothe Coco then began to think of her son and what lengthy prison time she faces. All her lost riches, lavish trips, expensive wardrobe and jewels seemed so insignificant now. With prison time imminent, she would lose it all.

At sentencing, Smoothe Coco received three years in a Texas Federal Prison. She was required to pay her own flight fees, court cost, attorney fees, and report to Federal Prison in 14 days. That meant she had to sell all her belongings to meet those requirements. The money left over was to help care for her son while she was in prison. If she failed to be in Texas at the Federal Bureau of Prisons on the exact day and time, she would be charged with prison escape and receive 5 years on top of the three. Avoiding prison was not an option. She now recognized the price of street fame…it's costly!

Coco's mother refused to take care of her son because it reminded her of the drug dealer who ruined her only child's life. The pain was to much to bear, so the childhood girl group Smoothe Coco had abandoned during her days as a dancer and baller stepped in to care for her son while she served time in a prison 1,349 miles from Detroit.

The choice of dancing in bars, compromising your body for cash, jewelry, clothes, or selling drugs for a certain lifestyle or to obtain a college education is self defeating. If that is your excuse, then what is your career goal? Who has been successful doing it that way and is able to sincerely talk positive about it? What you do today will definitely reflect on what you may become tomorrow. So if you don't want to be ashamed of the choices you make today, then live for tomorrow, by not making the wrong choices today.

Who Do You Believe In?

Self Empowerment is one of the most powerful qualities you possess as a human being. The ability within you to control your basic desires, determine your own destiny, and your willingness to achieve whatever positive results <u>you</u> desire, is self empowerment. It is also the ability <u>and</u> desire to exercise that power within you to make the sacrifices necessary for the benefit of your long term goals rather than immediate or temporary gratification.

You have the power within you to make the choices necessary and not be pressured or influenced by negative people, circumstances, the environment, or all of the other perceived obstacles that appear to direct or deter you from following your dreams and reaching your goals in life.

The aspirations you have as a child or teenager of being a Congress person, Computer Analysis, Accountant, Nurse, Teacher, Spelling Bee Champion, Physical Therapist, Fireman, Spiritual Leader, Policeman, Sports Announcer, Newspaper Writer, Scientist, Entrepreneur, Beautician, Baseball, Basketball, or Hockey Player – whatever career you desire, can be your gateway to fulfilling your life's purpose. My purpose is teaching!

You do have a purpose in life and you must treasure and direct your focus on achieving your dreams until they become your reality. Don't make or accept excuses nor sell your dreams short. You may encounter obstacles on your road of right choices, so acknowledge them as signs and be assured that just beyond that barrier is a milestone. When you have difficulty in achieving what you most desire, stay with it, because that may be a sign that you are on the correct path. Most things that come easy don't last very long. Whatever you want to achieve in life is going to require some form of sacrifice. That is, the giving up of something, going the extra mile for something, giving more of yourself than you're getting, or tolerating a person or situation that seems unbearable in order to continue forward in your goals.

The world is at your fingertips with all of the technology in this age of computers and instant messaging.

If you're receiving lessons in school you believe to be substandard or not interesting, then email or write your State Representative or State Senator and express your concerns. Go on your state's government website and request a "Citizens Guide to State Government." Learn who your legislators are. Get involved in State Government, Student Government, Student Council, and prepare yourself for your right to vote. If you don't have an organization to brainstorm and to develop your options, then show your leadership qualities and start one. Find a responsible, concerned adult who will help you create an after school program or think tank for like minded people such as yourself. Build an agenda through this workshop and present your student concerns. You have the power to direct your education and destiny. But, that's just another thing they may not tell you.

You are way more powerful as a student and a citizen than you believe. The fact of the matter is, you can make a difference. Make it a project to learn what your rights as a citizen may be. Challenge the school curriculum that isn't productive to the majority of the students. Do your research on the web, explore other options, and present your position intelligently. Decision makers can be convinced to listen once you present the facts.

Times are changing much faster than they were 5 or 10 years ago. You need to assist the decision-makers in your school, in your community, and in state and federal government to make the right choices <u>with</u> you. You have no idea of just how influential your voice can be as a young adult. That is another reason why I am calling on the higher potential within you. Your potential is just waiting to spring into action and explore all the possibilities that lie within this world.

I am calling her or him to task. You can feel the need growing within your breast and have the ability to direct it to be the leader your very nature demands. Make a sincere effort to accept this great responsibility and do your research in what sparks your interest. Gather all the information you can, and compare what you find on your interest to make the most informed decision possible. Know what path you need to take. Plan your journey from start to finish and account for the obstacles so you won't get discouraged or settle for anything less than success. "Most plans fail because you fail to plan." Learn from that truth…they may not tell you.

Moving past obstacles will build your confidence as well as your character. You will learn to deal with conflict in a positive way, and not resort to anger or frustration. Challenges along your journey will inspire you to challenge yourself and develop creative ways or alternative means in reaching your destination. They place you on notice and call to action the power you already possess once you accept the truth that you have this ability.

No outside force of circumstance, of situations, of family structure, of peer pressure. of failed school system or whatever other excuse available, can stop you from arriving. The Captain and Navigator of the ship is you. The Queen of the Castle is always home because you are that being. It is you who determines your destiny. It is you who can call forth the self-discipline necessary to avoid the negative influences of drugs, guns, street riches, violence, or whatever else that is counterproductive in achieving your fullest potential.

It is you and only you, with the guidance and love of like minded spirits who appreciate, recognize, encourage, and support you in your life's journey. It all begins with making right choices. Don't settle for the fake knockoffs of street life. You are much too valuable to play yourself for street life nickel and dimes. The millionaire potential inside of you is destined to make its appearance when you continue to make the right choice and follow the rules of your higher self.

    Believe in yourself and recognize your power of choice.
    David Keith Hudson, "an experienced courier"

About The Author

"If you take a man as he is, you make him worse than he was, but if you see him as being the best person possible, then he, in fact, becomes the best person possible…"

"See You At The Top"

Since David Hudson's 29 years or so, of incarceration he has made some significant strides in self improvement. He has married, maintained family and community ties, effective communication with his daughter Erica Iris, supporting her financially through hobbycraft sales, spiritually, and morally.

He has not been a perfect prisoner, and has made some mistakes early on along the way. However, compared to 90% of the prisoner population in Michigan, David may be considered a "model prisoner".

Although he is a Certified Health Educator, a Paralegal with an Associates Degree of College Credits in Business Administration. He has studied and continued to educate himself in these fields as well as other areas of self improvement to a fairly high degree.

David had never been in any trouble prior to incarceration, however he had issues which he failed to recognize and deal with. He was born onto a mother who was addicted to prescription drugs, he was physically and verbally abused, and by the age of 14 yrs old he was addicted to the same prescription drug Valium. He grew up without solid direction. So David ended up making the wrong choice <u>one</u> Saturday night and aided and abetted in the crimes of a robbery and murder that sent him to prison.

Community Action Porteros Inc., "CAPS Inc.", is compelled to say that David has come to terms and accepted responsibility for his actions or lack therof in the crime for which he was convicted. He has used that acceptance as motivation for self improvement and coupled with counseling gives us a reasonable assurance he is now capable of making more right choices.

- David has utilized his time actively pursing new aims, goals and objectives. In his senior year of high school he was one of 20 students throughout Detroit Public Schools selected for the Senior Intensified Program at Wayne State University. After graduating from Charles H. Chadsey High School in 1976, David eventually became certified as a Welder for the Ford Motor Company at the Rouge Stamping Plant following in his fraternal family roots, until the big layoffs in 1979. After this time he attended Marygrove College in the X-ray Technician Program. He later worked as a Mail Sorter in the U.S. Postal Service at Metro Airport in 1982-83. In 1983-84, he furthered his studies by enrolling in college full time prior to incarceration. David made the Dean's List while attending WCCC. He also worked as a Seasonal Vender at Tiger Stadium in Detroit, MI., and the Detroit Grand Prix. However since being incarcerated he has achieved additional education, skills and accomplishments to his repertoire. We will attempt to share a few.

- David completed individual sessions of counseling with Dr. Charles Harper, Psychologist, from 4/5/90 –

3/12/92. He was seen once per week for fifty minutes each session. According to Dr. Harper's termination report, *His use of therapy to foster personal growth in his life has been nothing short of phenomenal....Mr. Hudson has no personality disorder and if he is released from prison he can be expected to become a leader in his community and make a major positive contribution.*

- David was primary in organizing several Legislative Town Hall style meetings within the Michigan Penal System. State Senators and Representatives came into the prison system and took questions and answers from prisoners and listened to their concerns. This was an event that had never before took place in the Michigan Prison System. He has been the master of ceremony in townhall meetings at the Ryan, Gus Harrison and Lakeland Facilities annually from 2007 to the present. He has received a Deputy Warden's accommodation for his achievements for his well organized and intellectual programming.

- David has completed the 2 year Chance for Life Program ("CFL") and is a Core Member under the Leadership and Executive Direction of CFL, Millionaire Businessman Tom Adams and Ms. Jessica Taylor. CFL provides an intense curriculum which includes Mediation Training, Critical Thinking, Substance Abuse Counseling, Communication Skills, Conflict Resolution Training, etc. CFL is now in 8 Michigan prisons and has developed over the past 20 years. Mr. Adams has been a mentor to David as well as to an elite group of other prisoners throughout the state. CLF's motto is: "Be ye transformed by the renewing of your mind."

- Mr. Hudson Bey was instrumental in bringing the Inside Out Program in the Michigan Penal System under the supervision of Dr. Lori Lempert, University of Michigan Professor, Department of Behavioral Sciences. Inside Out is a national program that allows 15 university students to come into the prison setting and hold class with a carefully select group of inside students. David is in the follow up Therapy Group of the Inside Out Program which continues college course studies. These programs are still running in the Michigan system. Dr. Lempert is a longstanding "mentress" to David.

- On September 24, 2005, at the Ryan Road Facility, David was awarded a *Certificate of Appreciation* by The Wayne County Commission, Jewel Ware, Chair, District 4 and the NAACP Detroit Branch for his participation and achievements in various community programs and prison activities.

- The Greater Detroit, Michigan Chapter of Concerned Men Inc., awarded David a Certificate for his participation in a Male Responsibility and Fatherhood Development Program taught by Social Worker Kenny Anderson.

- Also while at the Ryan Correctional Facility, David made outstanding accomplishments and contributions in a Leadership Development Class in 2005 sponsored by the *Tree of Love Prison Ministry* with instructor Cardinal Mbiyu Chui (Rev. Moore).

- On November 29, 2004, while at the Macomb Correctional Facility, David successfully participated in and completed Anger Manager with Register Nurse Peggy Hanson, Instructor.

- On March 23, 2003, at the Saginaw Correctional Facility, David organized a Parole Workshop with the

American Friends Service Committee, Penny Ryder, Director.

- March 22, 2003, at the Saginaw Correctional Facility, David participated in the "Restorative Justice" Program with Alphonse Anderson, Director for the Shiawassee County Non Secure Detention Center for Juvenile Delinquent Court Wards between ages 10-17 years old. Judge James R. Clatterbaugh oversees this juvenile program. Mr. Hudson was a participant in the reality video taping to mentor children at risk.

- In 2002, while at the Saginaw Correctional Facility, Mr. Hudson helped publish the NAACP Newsletter and was on the Board of Directors at the Saginaw Institutional NAACP Branch. David served as the Religious Director where he organized various seminars with *Reconciliation of Life Ministry*, Sister Wanda Rogers Director. He helped raise donations to fund this worthwhile prison ministry. Mr. Hudson sponsored workshops with Dr. Manuel H. Pierson, Director of F.A.C.E.S. and publisher to *The Diaspora Speaks*. Also David organized annual Kwanzaa Celebration Programs, CO-founded *Father's Incarcerated Needing to be Dad F.I.N.D., Inc.,* and published the "Redball Express" Newsletters. Fathers Incarcerated is a grassroots nonprofit organization aimed at reuniting Dads with their children and make charitable contribution to homeless and abuse shelters. He futhered his education in the English 212 Communication Program with Dr. Phyllis Hastings, Saginaw Valley University Professor. He has published material through many higher learning programs.

- David obtained high scores in earning his paralegal certification from The Blackstone School of Law in 2001. He was also the President and Legal Assistant for the National Lifer's of America Inc., (NLA) Chapter #1020, Lapeer MI. This is a National Lifer Organization that champion prisoner's rights. He published the *Other Side Newsletter* which is a prisoner publication created to inform the public on prison issues and related events.

- David organized and spearheaded other Legal Workshops as NLA'S #1020 President hosted by prominent attorneys such as Laura Kathleen Sutton (Manchester, MI), Jeanice Dagher-Margosian (AnnArbor, MI), Rosemary Gordon (Grosse Pointe, MI), and Brendan T. Beery (Lansing, MI). These workshops were organized to educate NLA members and the general population on changes in the law, behind the scenes of the court system, and effective brief writing. David also organized two major Parole workshops for the entire Thumb Correctional Facility General Population hosted by American Friends Service Committee Director Ms. Penny Ryder and a previous Program Associate Shelley Anzalone. These workshops helped prepare TCF staff and prisoners for Parole Board Hearings, Lifer Reviews and Release. In addition, he organized a Mandatory Sentencing Workshop hosted by Families Against Mandatory Minimums (FAMM) past Michigan Project Director, past Michigan Jewish Conference Director and previous CAPPS Secretary, Susan R. Herman. This workshop educated the general population on the history and drawbacks of mandatory sentences.

- David has written several articles/essays, which have been published by various newspapers and magazines. His monthly writings can be reviewed in the defunct Thumb Print Newspaper. With the elimination of prison newspapers, The Otherside News, Fathers Incarcerated and the NAACP Newsletters have become primary sources of prisoner rights issues for legal professionals, community leaders, politicians and prisoners alike.

EDUCATIONAL:

- During Mr. Hudson's early years at Jackson's Central Complex (SMI), he attended Jackson Community College where he made outstanding achievements and earned various college credits in **Data Processing, Intro. to the Legal System, Legal Research, Wellness, Computer Programming, Intro. to Business, Accounting, Business Communication, Advertising, Principles of Retailing, General Biology, etc.,**

- The State of Michigan Department of Public Health sponsored a HIV Counseling and Testing Training course, which David participated and was certified as a HIV/AIDS Peer Educator, while housed at the Western Wayne Correctional Facility. Being a HIV/AIDS Peer Educator his responsibilities were to give a biweekly presentation to all incoming technical & parole violators on the importance of safe sex and prevention. This presentation was given by David and another qualified prisoner who received state certification in completing the course. David spearheaded the question and answer session with one on one consultation throughout the facility on HIV-AIDS education, prevention and contraction. This was a very fulfilling occupation for Mr. Hudson because it truly gave him the opportunity to give something meaningful back to the community at large. He was very pleased with the experience and the benefits achieved. *All client consultation is confidential.*

- In addition to writing a play for the U of M Drama Club with Professor Buzz Alexander, David helped establish various drug education programs at Western Wayne Correctional along with several staff members. It was his responsibilities to show videos and hold open forum discussions with all incoming prisoners who were required to participate in the drug programs. David worked with WWCF Administrators to establish the most effective programs for the men returning to prison on parole and technical violations. This volunteer assignment was self-fulfilling and educational.

- Dean Edwynna R. Dansby at Schoolcraft College, Livonia MI, certified Mr. Hudson as a Custodial Service Representative.

- The Jaycee of Kinross Correctional sponsored a Substance Abuse Awareness Program in which David successfully completed.

- A Special Substance Abuse Program was offered at the Adrian Correctional Facility sponsored by Family Service & Children's Aid (FSCA) is a community based Substance Treatment Program. David completed this program on his own initiative with excellent attendance, participation, and met all treatment and educational objectives.

- Mr. Hudson successfully achieved the high standard of excellence in Artist Management Classes and was awarded a Certificate of Achievement at the Adrian Correctional Facility.

- Other achievements during the same period at Adrian Correctional were: *Certification of Academic Achievement* for successfully completing an elective course from the **Department of English Sienna Heights College** entitled What is Woman Part 1 & 2 by **Patricia Schnapp Ph.D.**

- Dr. George Moss, Professor University of Michigan, Flint MI, and Professor at Mott College taught ancient Egyptian History classes Mr. Hudson attended and completed. He participated in the Legal Research Workshop Program at TCF with certification.

- State Representative Derrick Hale sponsored Mr. Hudson in receiving certification from the State of Michigan as a Notary Public. David held office as a Notary until the law was repealed.

- Not only has Mr. Hudson been successful in improving and strengthening his mental, spiritual, emotional, and psychological well being, he has remained physically fit. David has promoted and competed in numerous physical competitions (5K & 10K Runs, Volleyball, Tennis, Handball, Weightlifting, etc.) with high levels of success and achievements.

Conclusion:

David's decades of incarceration has been spent on self improvement, the litigation of prisoners rights and the bettering of conditions in – not only prison, but in the outside communities as well. Mr. Hudson also spent considerable time and effort learning to understand the spiritualities of life. He is a better person because of it. Although he has hit some bumps along the way, David has kept his feet on the path of habilitation and his goals above his present circumstances.

David maintains regular contact with his daughter and two daughters through marriage, assisting them morally and financially. He sold leather craft items to fund Erica a trip to Disney World when she was just 10 years old. He provided for her high school graduation cost among many other daily needs. Erica never allowed David to use prison as an excuse not to be her father and provide for her care. Watching his daughters grow up from inside prison has been one of the most difficult parts of his incarceration. Living through his mother, father and brother's death has been another challenging portion of incarceration. He understands what his victim's family must be experiencing. Michigan Prisoner #A179401 made a choice. Mr. Hudson accept responsibility for his role in this crime. He has the support of family and friends to aid him in his transition back into the community.

David has helped several people during his prison term and has shown tremendous progress toward habilitation. He has given his daughters as well as other young adults guidance and has diligently tried to instill a sense of morals, social duties, and responsibilities in the people he meets. Mr. Hudson has enhanced the skills he came to prison with and has gained many additional useful skills that can be applied productively in society. In our long term observation, David has learned from his mistakes and became a better man capable of being a productive citizen.

David has endorsements and commendable letters of his sentencing Judge Francis X O'Brien, his successor Chief Circuit Court Judge Wendy Potts, United States District Judge Avern Cohn, Senator Michael Switalski, Attorney Jeanice Dagher Margosian, Judge Bruce Morrow, Attorney Brian Lawson, University of Michigan Professors, and others. You may concede, David made the choice to change his life. This book is also a testimony to that change.

Community Action Porteros Inc.

Special Thanks

To all of my surogate mothers who taught me that it really does take a village to raise a child. You have nurtured me and supported me through all my trials and tribulations. I can not convey my humble appreciation enough for your undying patience and unconditional love: LaGloria Roberts, Mother Lucille Steele, Sister Julia Hervey, Shirley Harp-Davidson. And the other mothers "In Memory of" whom god has chosen to sit by his side. Thank you for taking the role you promised Rosie Hudson you would fulfill after she passed. I am forever grateful because of you all (you all are the greatness in me).

To Bishop William Murphy III, and the New Mt. Moriah family, ,you have been a greater inspiration and supporter to me than you can ever imagine. When we were just teenagers and I was learning how to drive, you and the other young ministers trusted me to chauffeur you around Detroit to various churches and I am grateful for your continued belief and faith in me. Your prayers have been my foundation to turn my life around and make better choices; Sheik Craig Fuqua Bey and the members of the Moorish Science Temple of America #25, Detroit, Mich., you've shown me what a "reformed man" can accomplish; to the Washitnaw Muurs; to Pastor Ocie Tubb; to the New Salem Baptist Church, thanks for your support; to Deacon Joseph Lateef, you've "Been there, done that".

To my "Soul Brothers" Kevin (Bowers) Miah, Stanley Blakely and Jerry Hessel, thank you for reaching back when you were released.

To Kelvin "Lil Bird" Judkins El, thank you for reaching back showing me that my efforts to save just one young man was not in vain.

To Antoine "Tiny" Thomas Bey, you were only sixteen years old when you ran away from Califonia to spend most of your life in a Michigan prison. Thank you for accepting me as your mentor and developing into the leader you were destined to be. You took back your power of choice and didn't allow your family past to determine your destiny. You gave me the inspiration to sincerely believe I can truly make a difference in a young man's life. Let's get back to writing your life story.

To Detroit Free Press Editorial Writer Jeff Gerritt, for all your articles and support on prisoner programs and rights.

To the Inglewood Urban prep Campus, Chicago Illinois, for giving young men the hope and preparation for College.

To Kwame "The Mayor" Kilpatrick, you told me they were trying to lock you up. "Surrendered" is proof your time was well spent.

In Memory Of...

To the victims of my wrong choices and actions, (crimes). I have taken everything from you and your family without the means to replacing it. Please forgive me? No matter how much time I serve, my debt to society is non redeemable. Only God can clear my debt.

My father, John Henry. You have been my role model since the very first day Dr. Martin slapped my bottom and I cried out. I apologize for deviating from your plan. My mother Rosie Mae. I gave you your flowers while you could smell them, caused you pain from your varicose veins to your congestive heart failure. My wrong choice that cold January night was not your fault. You were the best mother you knew how to be. My brother Johnnie Earl. You were my idol and best friend. You know the world isn't any safer with me being locked up. "True brotherhood eternally. They can't stop the official".

All the spirits that have crossed over into the plane of Soul during my incarceration: "The Old Pro" A/K/A Robert Taylor, Mother in Law Louise Taylor, Brother in Law Michael Jeffery Taylor, Edgar Brazelton, Jr. (Brazelton's Florist), Uncle John C. Hudson, Uncle Booker T. Price, Uncle Herman T. Taylor, Sister in law Rita Olivia Jones-Hudson, Sister in Law A Hudson, Allen Leon Roberts, Anthony Durr Roby, Darrell Duane Roby, Cousin Bruce Edwin Hervey, Cousin Donald "Duck" Everett Taylor, Cousin Kathy Elizabeth Price, Cousin Wilma Alice Maples, Mammie Johnson,

Florence Wallace Davidson, Charles David Davidson, Verna Mae Hoover, Booker T. Hoover, Dorothy "Peaches" Crowder, Annie "Big Momma" McCall, Mother Grace Wallace, Mother A. Brown, Melvin Cook, Sis Myrene Burnette Caldwell, Miquel Jerome "Man" Brown, Cathy Hines, John "Johnny" T. Grimes, Dominique Lamont Conrad (1992-2010), Biz, Alredo X, Gross El, Mays Bey, Skip "Murder" X, Judge Francis X. O'Brien.

Printed in Great Britain
by Amazon.co.uk, Ltd.,
Marston Gate.